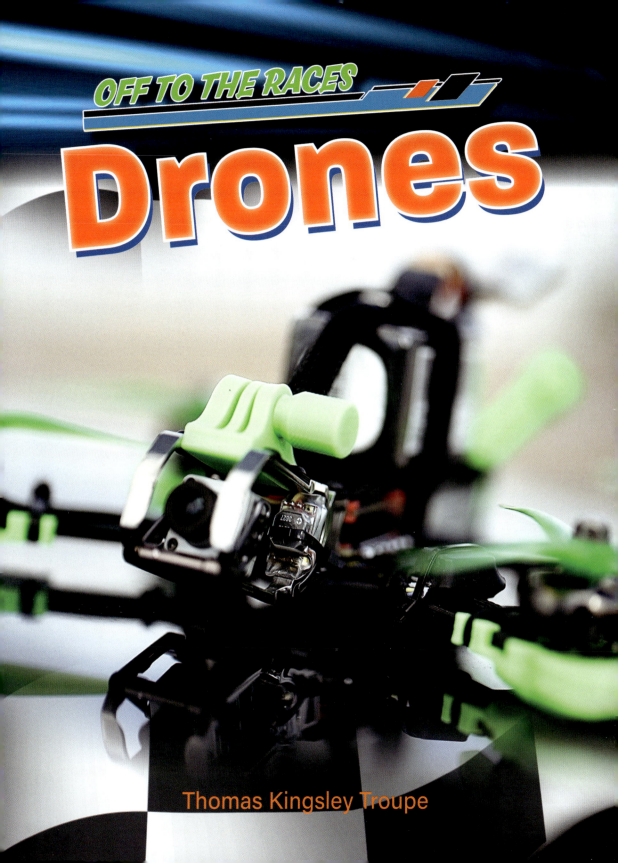

# OFF TO THE RACES

# Drones

Thomas Kingsley Troupe

## 45th Parallel Press

Published in the United States of America by Cherry Lake Publishing Group
Ann Arbor, Michigan
www.cherrylakepublishing.com

Reading Adviser: Beth Walker Gambro, MS, Ed., Reading Consultant, Yorkville, IL

PHOTOS CREDITS: ©www.shutterstock.com Cover: ©shutterstock/Ruslan Sitarchuk, Title ©Stefanetti Emmanuel, Page 2 ©shutterstock Ruslan Sitarchuk, Page 3 ©Abcdef, page 4 ©Goinyk Production, page 5 ©vaalaa, page6-7 ©MONOPOLY919, Page 7 ©Scharfsinn, page 8 ©Red Fox studio, page8 ©shutterstock, page 8-9 ©WESTOCK PRODUCTIONS, page 10 ©RZ Images, page 11 ©SolidMaks, page 12-13 ©Phatphum Phetchakan, page 12 ©SolidMaks, page 13 ©aerogondo2, page 14 ©Luis Molinero, page 15 ©Stefanetti Emmanuel, page 16 © Andrei Stepanov, page 17 ©Kietisak Yaemklebbua, page 18 ©Yankovsky88, page19 ©Rayna Grace page, 20 ©BorneoJC James, Yanosh Nemesh, page 21-23-25 ©Melanie Wallner (CCA Share 4.0 https://creativecommons.org/licenses/by-sa/4.0), page 22 ©Yanosh Nemesh, page 24 ©byvalet, page, 25 ©teve Paston, page 25 b©Pixel-Shot, Page 26 ©socrates471, page 28 ©stock image, page 29 ©Dmyers86 (CCA Share 4.0 https://creativecommons.org/licenses/by-sa/4.0), page 30 ©Simply Amazing, page 31 ©Allahfoto. ©www.dreamstime.com

Produced for Cherry Lake Publishing by bluedooreducation.com

Copyright © 2026 by Cherry Lake Publishing Group

All rights reserved. No part of this book may be reproduced or utilized in any form or by any means without written permission from the publisher.

**45th Parallel Press** is an imprint of Cherry Lake Publishing Group.

Library of Congress Cataloging-in-Publication Data has been filed and is available at catalog.loc.gov.
Printed in the United States of America

Note from Publisher: Websites change regularly, and their future contents are outside of our control. Supervise children when conducting any recommended online searches for extended learning opportunities.

## ABOUT THE AUTHOR

*Thomas Kingsley Troupe is the author of over 300 books for young readers. When he's not writing, he enjoys reading, playing video games, and hunting ghosts as part of the Twin Cities Paranormal Society. Otherwise, he's probably taking a nap or something. TKT lives in Woodbury, MN, with his two sons.*

# Table of Contents

**CHAPTER 1**
Introduction............................................4

**CHAPTER 2**
The Race Is On!...................................... 8

**CHAPTER 3**
Drone Racing Pilots............................. 14

**CHAPTER 4**
Drone Racing Events...........................22

Did You Know?.....................................30
Find Out More......................................32
Glossary ................................................32
Index......................................................32

# Chapter 1
# Introduction

There's a strange sound outside. It sounds like humming or buzzing. It's not a giant insect. It's a drone! Drones have spinning blades. They move very fast. They create a humming sound.

Batteries give drones their power.

United States Air Force drone in 2016

Drones are UAVs. UAV means unmanned **aerial** vehicle. Aerial means in the air. Drones are controlled **remotely**. Remotely means from a distance. The pilot does not have to be near the drone to fly it. The military used drones first. Today, people use drones more and more. They can help with tasks. No wonder drones are just about everywhere!

Farmers and ranchers use drones. A drone's camera can help them. They can see all of their crops. They can monitor their animals from the sky.

   Drones can help save lives. They assist in search and rescue missions. Photographers can take aerial photos from the sky. Delivery drones can deliver packages. It helps make shipping faster!

   Drones are creating new jobs. They are used for business solutions. Drones can help almost every **industry**, or area of business.

## Chapter 2
# The Race Is On!

Racing drones is a new sport. It started over 12 years ago. High-tech drones are fast and **agile**. Agile means it can make quick moves. Tech-racing lovers found the perfect racers!

The first official U.S. drone race was in 2014. Soon after, many **organizations**, or groups, were formed. They wanted to support the exciting sport of drone racing.

Drones were fast. Drone engineers made them faster! Some drones fly up to 70 miles (110 kilometers) per hour. Racing drones are even faster. They can fly 100 mph (160 km/h)!

Drones can be different shapes. Some have 3 propellers. Others have 4 or more. Drones come in many sizes too.

Drone builders are always making improvements. They try to make them quicker. Someday drones will reach unbelievable speeds. They could fly over 200 mph (321 km/h)!

Drones can be found in stores everywhere. Speed upgrades can turn a drone into a racer.

Early drones were heavy. The first military UAV weighed over 200 pounds (90.71 kilograms). Today they are lightweight. A larger drone weighs around 44 pounds (19.9 kgs).

Drones can be tiny. Micro drones are around 2 inches (5 centimeters) wide. Micro drones have racing events. These little drones can hit speeds of 40 mph (64 km/h).

The bigger the battery, the longer the flight! Bigger drones fly longer and faster. Their big batteries give them enough power. Smaller drones have smaller batteries. That means shorter flights.

**Micro drone**

## Chapter 3
# Drone Racing Pilots

Some drones can fly on their own. They are **programmed** to control themselves. When something is programmed, it means someone wrote computer code. The code, or programming, tells the drone what to do. Racing drones are different. They need a skilled flier. These fliers are called pilots. Good pilots can fly drones fast.

A pilot uses a controller to fly a drone. The pilot also wears FPV or first-person view goggles. The goggles use a **wireless** connection to the drone's camera. Wireless means they can operate without wires. The camera lets the pilot see through the drone's eyes.

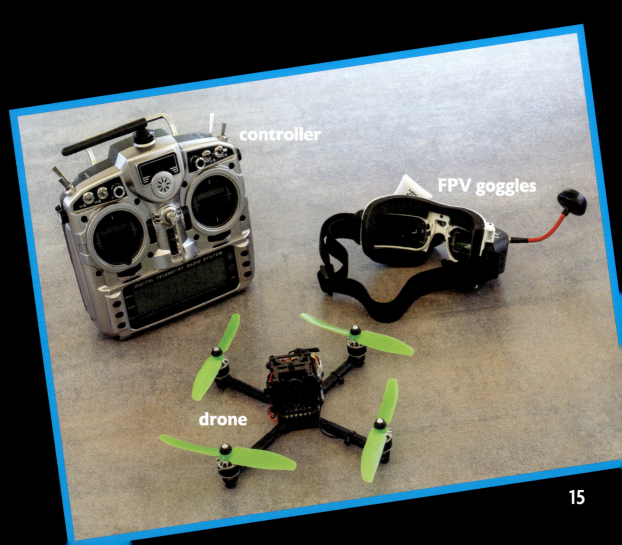

15

Using FPV goggles is strange at first. It makes some people dizzy. New pilots should start by sitting down. It can take time to adjust to the goggles.

The pilot needs to be in the drone's range. The devices need to **communicate**, or exchange messages, with each other. Radio Frequency (RF) signals connect the goggles, controller, and drone together.

RF Waves

antenna

RF signals are everywhere! Cell phones, WiFi, and GPS rely on RF signals. They need them to work. Most devices have hidden antennas.

RF signals are **electromagnetic waves**. These are a type of energy. They can carry information. All of the devices have antennas. They are used to receive and send RF signals.

antenna

# The Controller

The controller connects the pilot and drone. The pilot's skills guide the controller. Together, the pilot and the controller work like the drone's brain. They tell the drone what to do.

> The Drone Racing League and the U.S. Air Force work together. The program helps recruit pilots for the military. Now that's an impressive partnership!

# The Pilot

Skilled pilots win races. Pilots can move up into competitive racing. Competitive racing offers prize money and trophies. A skilled pilot and a fast drone have the right stuff to win!

Racing drones at top speeds is tricky. It takes a lot of skill. Great pilots have amazing hand-eye **coordination**. Coordination means parts of the body work together well. Practice helps improve this skill!

Ready to race? Join a local racing club. Start one if there is not one near you! Over time, you could build a league of pilots.

Pilots spend hours and hours training. They fix their devices often. Pilots will also tweak their equipment. They want to make their racers better!

## Chapter 4
# Drone Racing Events

Drone races can take place indoors or outdoors. Outdoor races can be affected by weather.

Drone racing is a worldwide sport. The Drone Racing League holds events nearly everywhere! Pilots compete all over North America, Asia, Europe, and Africa.

Lights out? Some indoor drone races happen in the dark. LED lights brighten the course and the drones. The LEDs help the pilots and crowd watch the race. Indoor drone racing is loud…but colorful!

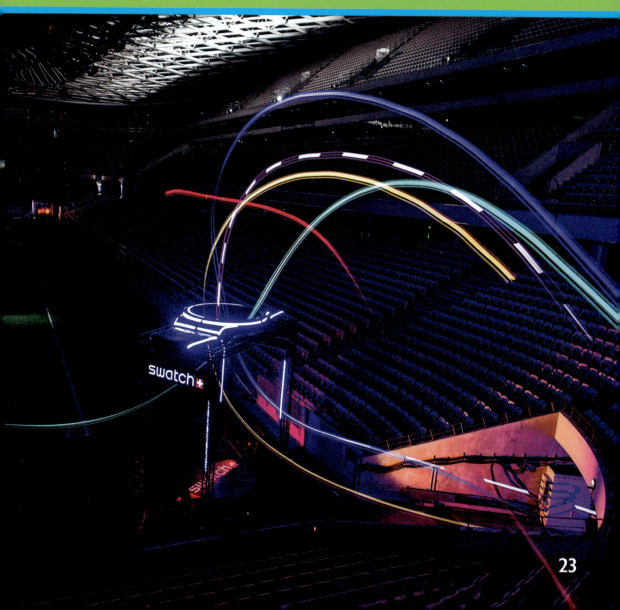

Indoor and outdoor drone racing rules are the same. The pilots fly their drones around the course. They need to be faster than the other pilots.

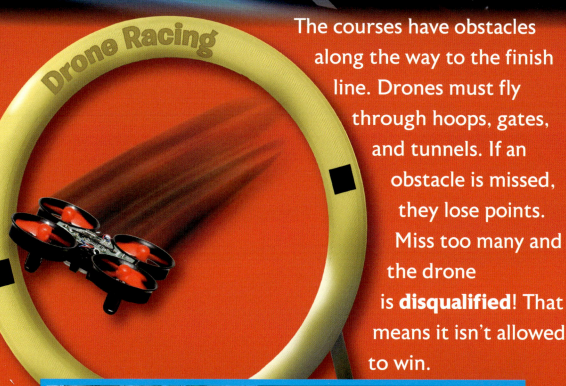

Drone Racing

The courses have obstacles along the way to the finish line. Drones must fly through hoops, gates, and tunnels. If an obstacle is missed, they lose points. Miss too many and the drone is **disqualified**! That means it isn't allowed to win.

25

Drone racing takes quick thinking. Pilots need to react fast. Both of these skills help them stay on course. Pilots should also avoid crashing into other drones!

## Do It Yourself!

Try designing a practice course! It can be as long or short as you want. You can buy drone gates and pylons. But you can also make your own!

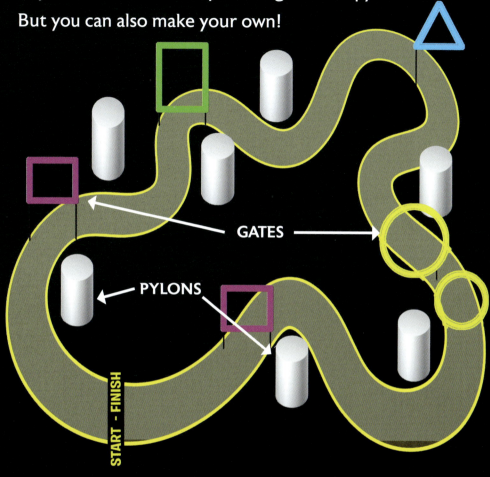

## General Course Rules:

- Most races are scored with points. More points mean victory!
- Pilots earn points by navigating obstacles. Missed one? Pilots can turn around and try again.
- Avoid penalties! Points can be lost for pilots who break rules. Early starts, crashes, and flying too high earn penalties. Too many broken rules can lead to being disqualified.
- Speed is important. Slow drones get left in the dust...or clouds!

**TOP RACING ORGANIZATIONS:**
- Drone Racing League (DRL)
- United States Air Force (USAF)
- MultiGP Drone Racing League (MultiGP)
- Major League Drone Racing (MLDR)
- Drone Champions League (DCL)

Top racing organizations hold competitions. They want to find out who is the best. The organizers design the courses. Many competitions supply the racing drones. This means pilots all use the same kind of drone. No drone is built faster than another. It keeps the competition fair.

It takes practice to win races. The courses are tough and the other pilots want to win! Is drone racing for everyone? There's only one way to find out. Fire up the drone and get flying! Off to the races!

# Did You Know?

Drones use Radio Frequencies (RF). This helps them communicate. Flying a drone with FPV goggles is different. It needs 2-way wireless communication. That means it needs 2 channels. Each channel is on a different frequency. One frequency controls the drone. The other frequency sends video to the goggles.

Use 2.4 GHz frequency for the drone controller.
A 5.8 GHz can down-link to the FPV. If this is confusing, ask a pro!

*GHz stands for gigahertz. It is a unit of frequency.*

**Drone control down-link 5.8 GHz**

**Drone control up-link 2.4 GHz**

# What's inside a drone?

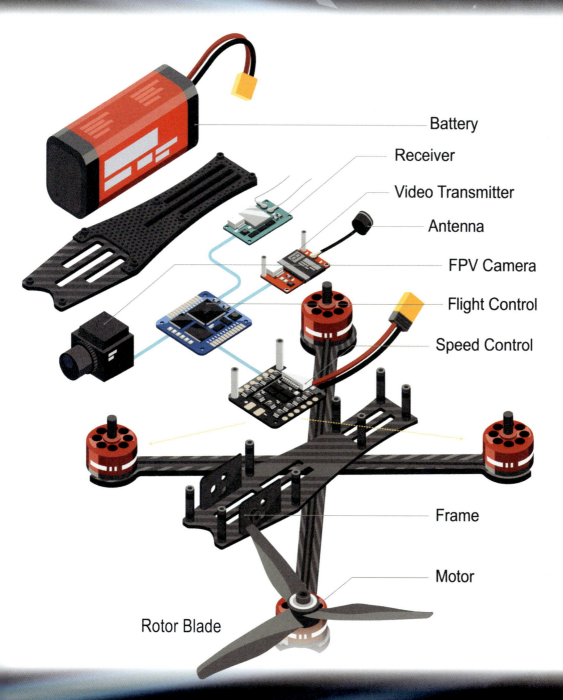

# Find Out More

**BOOKS**

Rathburn, Betsy. *Drones*. Minnetonka, MN: Bellwether Media, 2021.

Ringstad, Arnold. *What's Inside a Drone?* Mankato, MN: The Child's World, 2020.

**WEBSITES**

Search these online sources with an adult:

Drones | Kiddle

Drones | PBS Kids

# Glossary

**aerial** (AIR-ee-uhl) happening in the air

**agile** (AJ-ile) able to move fast and easily

**communicate** (kuh-MYOO-nih-kayt) to share information with

**coordination** (koh-or-duh-NAY-shuhn) ability to use different body parts to complete a task easily

**disqualified** (dis-KWAH-luh-fyed) not allowed to win

**electromagnetic waves** (ih-LEK-troh-mag-NET-ik WAYVS) waves of energy that travel at different wavelengths; include radio waves, light waves, and X-rays, among others

**industry** (IN-duh-stree) a single branch of business

**organizations** (or-guh-nuh-ZAY-shuhnz) different groups of people joined together for a particular purpose

**programmed** (PROH-gramd) given instructions to work in a certain way

**remotely** (rih-MOHT-lee) from a distance

**wireless** (WYE-uhr-luhs) not requiring wires to send or receive information

# Index

battery, 13, 31

communicate, 16, 30
competition(s), 28
controller, 15-16, 18, 30
course(s), 23-29

FPV, 15-16, 31
frequencies, 17, 30

gates, 25, 27
gigahertz, 30
goggles, 15, 16, 30

indoor(s), 22-24

micro drone(s), 12-13

organizations, 8, 28

pilot(s), 5, 14-16, 18-24, 26-29

rules, 24, 27

speed(s), 10-12, 20, 27, 31

UAV(s), 5, 12